AF392686

The Tidy-Up Tale of Tommy:

Cleaning up after oneself

LEGAL NOTICE

https.//harrywheat.com

Introduction

Tommy is a playful little boy who loves his toys, but he never wants to put them away. One day, his toys decide they've had enough and create a mess all on their own! As Tommy navigates through the chaos, he discovers a magical world of helpful little creatures who teach him the joys of tidying up. Through their friendship, Tommy learns that cleaning can be fun, and when everyone pitches in, it's even better.

Characters

- **Tommy**: A lively and imaginative boy who loves to play but struggles with cleaning up.

- **The Tidbits**: Magical, tiny creatures who delight in organizing and tidying up; they become Tommy's friends and guide him in learning how to clean.

- **Tommy's Mom**: Always encouraging Tommy to keep his room clean, she is kind and patient.

Cleaning up doesn't have to be a chore—it can be an enjoyable activity, especially when shared with friends.

Tommy loved his toys, scattered far and wide. From blocks to cars, they spread side to side.

But when the day ended, they weren't in their place, and tidying up came with quite the race!

"I'll clean it tomorrow," young Tommy would plead, as the toys piled up like tiny toy trees!

One special night, when the stars did not glout, Tommy's toys took their chance, and tiptoed about.

They twirled and they flipped, they jumped and they swung, making more mess, until the room spun!

Tommy woke up to a sea of clutter, toys everywhere, what a splutter!

In the middle of it all, a sight to surprise, tiny Tidbits buzzed like cheerful little flies.

"We're the Tidbits," they chimed, "and we're here to assist! Let's teach you to clean, you won't want to resist!"

"Together we'll stack, we'll sort and we'll sweep, making tidying a game that's fun and neat!"

With a giggle and a jump, Tommy joined in too, picking up toys with a new dance move.

They sang as they cleaned, a tune
oh so jolly, stacking and dusting
without any folly.

The room became tidy, a wonderful sight, sparkling with cheer and pure delight.

As the sun set, the Tidbits began to disappear, fading into the night with one last cheer.

Tommy beamed and marveled at the scene, realizing that tidying was not mean.

Job Well
Done Chart

Now every night, with a smile on his face, he tidies his room, loving his spa.

Toys
Toy
Toyss
Your Toy
Toy

His mom popped in, a smile big and wide, "Well done, Tommy," she'd say with pride.

Tommy learned that with effort, cleaning was fun, a lesson for everyone under the sun!

Clean Room
Achievements

From blocks to cars, his treasures now shone, with Tommy the Tidy leading the show.

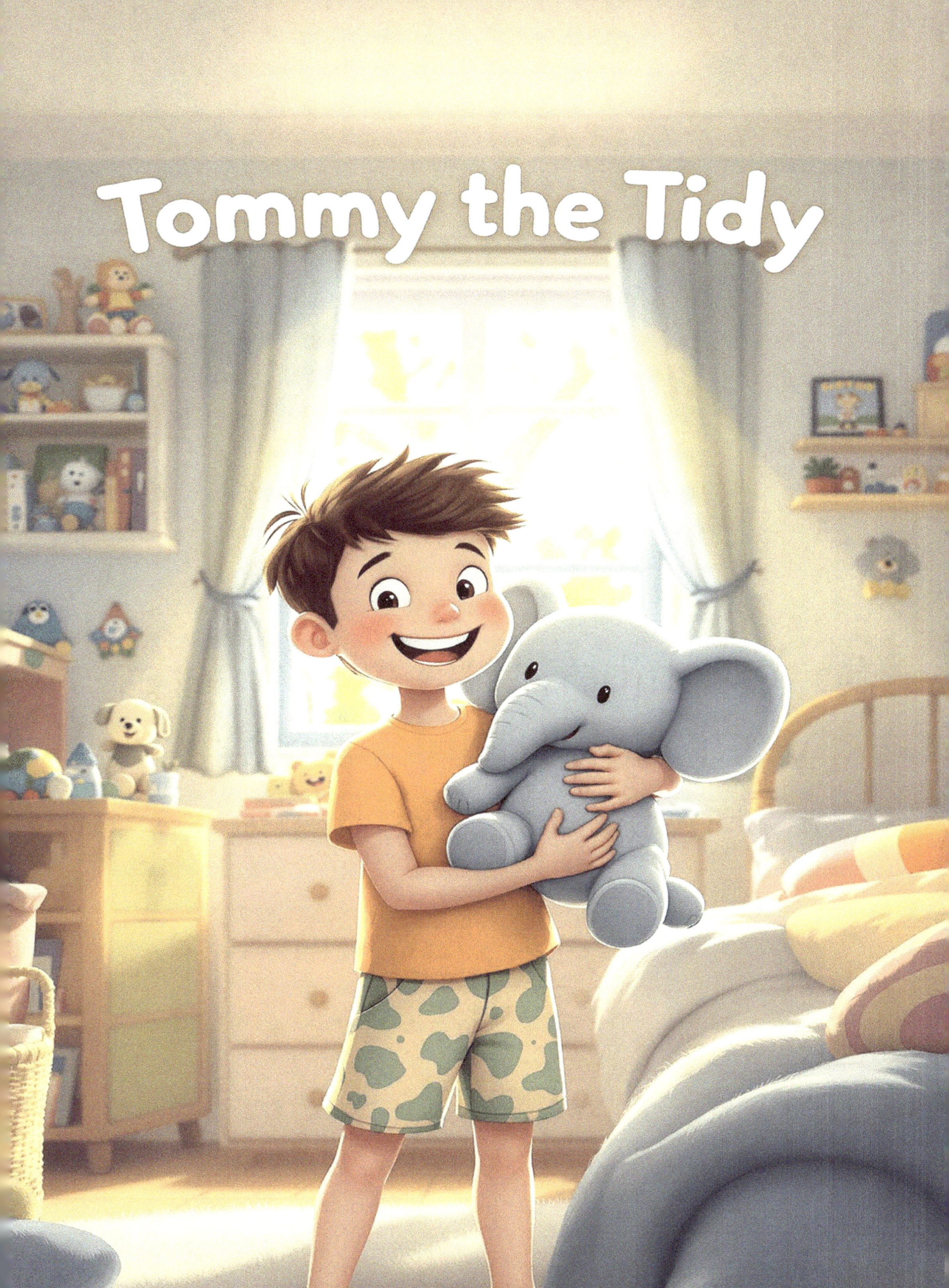
Tommy the Tidy

So remember, little one, wherever you roam, tidying up makes a house feel like home.

With a dash of magic and a sprinkle of fun, tidying's an adventure for everyone!